Operation

Digital

Boss

By: Marquise Rodgers

Published by: Dropbackdistro

2017

This book is
dedicated

To the

Memory

Of

Pamela A. Rodgers

Table of Contents

Introduction

In today's world being an entrepreneur is becoming very technical and advanced. If you don't know the ins and outs of the new digital industry you will be left behind and lost. Do you ever ask yourself "how did they do that", when it comes to marketing or just simple online business tolls such as social media, Websites or blogs. If so then this is the perfect book for you. This is the 123 guide into the digital business word.

I have marketed products for a variety of industries from music, to clothing and even the gaming industry. I've made a lot of extra income online now I'm able to share my secrets and strategies to digital entrepreneurship. I own Dawhoop Magazine, GoDream Media, and DropbackDistro the publishing company bringing you this book. As you can see things are working for me but enough about me let's get logged on!!!!

Chapter.1 Start Ups

Unlike most business startups, starting an online business is not as expensive as most startups depending on the industry that you choose to join. A good $2000 budget for online business startups would be great. This is for a great website design most website developers range from $300 to $500. You need good business cards to let potential clients know about your business. This will range anywhere from $20 to $100 depending on the graphic work you want on the cards.

You're going to need Fliers regardless of what most would like you to believe that fliers don't work anymore because of social media, but I'm here to tell you that's a lie. The truth is you're not friends with everyone on social media. Fliers will add value to your campaign add your social media info to the flier. This gives people something to remember you by.

I mentioned social media in the last paragraph believing that you have social media accounts. If you don't go ahead and build your pages on all relevant platforms. Now, that you have social media for your brand build it. Contrary to what people say buying followers and plays on video advertisement are common practice in all industries.

You might be asking yourself "Why". Well it's all about smoke and mirrors the old trick of the eye, remember what people see and hear is what the mind perceives. If you have 10k followers or over 10k plays on your videos people feel like they are late to the party. They want know what all the hype is about, and If you already have clients they want to show your company off to their friends and family. Obtain a business address and business license unlike social media which is a free promotional tool.

Now, I know what you are thinking how I am going to get a commercial property with a $2000 budget. On top of the fact that you have already spent money on promotional items. It's simple rent a business address downtown in your city. It's a lot of businesses that will rent you a business address with a mail receiving service and conference rooms available for meetings. Depending on your needs office space can range anywhere from $75 to $150 a month.

Start Up Map

- Get your address
- License your business
- Create your Social Media

- Create your Website
- Create your Business cards
- Design your Fliers

And now that your all setup the rule to this game is don't think it's get rich quick. You have to work nothing happens overnight.

Chapter.2 Benefits of the Digital Office

As I mentioned in the last chapter when I spoke about renting an address this is a term that many use in the digital industry. You can look online and search for towers in your town these are called business hubs. Plain and simple as long as you have your address you can license your business and operate it from anywhere with a Wi-Fi connection. This includes your favorite coffee shop, the library, school, restaurants, and we can't forget about my personal favorite your very own home. Now im saying quit your day job that a mistake I see a lot of people making even I have made the same mistake.

Quitting your job before you make profit off your business is not wise. The object of your business is to compete with your job. If your business is not making what your job is paying it's not time to quit yet. This is the benefit of having a digital office you can work it anytime of the day. The digital office keeps your family happy, it's easy on the pockets and you can have meetings in provided conference rooms or offices so you can keep your professional look.

Just look on your favorite search engines and search for Virtual Office Space for rent. Go ahead and secure your business office space today.

Chapter.3 Benefits of your Website

Now I can say a lot of extra words and go on and on about useless nothing talking about your website. I'm not here to confuse you like a lot of people try to do in other books. I'm going to get right to the meat of it. It's called "Monetizing Your Links", and now any link that you monetize becomes an advertisement link. Whenever someone clicks on it an advertisement pops up and you get paid. Did you know that well now you do and if you do you are ahead of the game?

To drive business to your site you can advertise on your site for other companies. This is called "Affiliate Marketing", now I told you that my company promoted products for major companies this is how. Many of your favorite companies have affiliate marketing programs were they pay you a percent of a sale that you send to them. Some also pay you per click this is called a lead and these are the best form to get paid by having a website.

That's not even the products and services that you are providing that's just extra income just from having a site. Now I'm going to get into that on and on talk about stuff you already know. You know the things your site designer already asked you lol just a little digital boss humor. You know all the basic info that should be on the site, products, contact info, etc. ...

Monetizing your links and affiliates marketing can bring big checks. Some even in the thousands advertisers pay a lot of money every year to get their products to the same people your trying to reach. You can help each other out kind of like a digital buddy system. This is the most valuable benefit of having a website that people don't tell you and make sure your site is powered by a global cdn which make your site really global and faster.

Chapter.4 Go Viral On Social Media Platforms

Ever since they gave us social media they have been giving us viral videos, viral photos and viral post help people gain national exposure for their brand. The average person might make a funny video or post and go viral by a miracle but you are a business you want the same effect. What people think of as a viral video or post is really an advertisement. A business pays a marketing firm for enough advertisement slots on social media to make this free tool really work for you.

Now combine with a go viral firm like HollyHam Media who has dedicated people on their staff across the globe who shares your product to their page human robots who job is to be connected to their computer all day. This method together with advertisement slots will gain you the viral success you seek for your brand.

It's not by luck you create your own luck in the digital world. Regular ordinary people never try to go viral it just happens but as a business you want to create the same effect over and over again. This can easily be done with the right firm and ad promo budget that you still have in your $2000 plan.

Buy followers, buy shares, buy likes all of this helps the smoke and mirror illusion. If your product already looks like it went viral then 9 times out of 10 it will go viral. Knowledge of social media can make you a magician and if you learn all the tricks you can do magic. Get with a firm today and check out your social media site advertisement prices.

Chapter.5 Meet the People

Social media is great but it can't help you gain personal relationships. Earlier in chapter.1 business startups I spoke about business cards and fliers. With your business being online and have a digital office you have more time to get out and promote your site and services. The business cards and fliers give you a reason to get to meet new people.

Let's be real if a stranger walks up to you and starts talking you will get very irritated and you might look at the crazy. Now, if I have business cards and fliers it gives people visuals, and something to talk about and gets that individuals interest in the conversation. If you have a good pitch for your product you will win a new client and that's what you want.

A good pitch only takes a good 30 to 60 seconds. You can go on and on about your products and services and people will lose interest. Think of it as a commercial on the radio or TV it's so short that people want more. If the client leaves wanting more information than they are going to get more information.

All in all you make money from them coming to view your site even if it's not with you. From shopping with you, clicking on links or shopping with one of your affiliates marketing partners. Let's get to working on your success plan called Operation Digital Boss and remember meeting people is the most important part of your business. They are your customers if you don't have any customers you don't have a business.

Terms to Remember

- Virtual Office
- Business License
- Social Media
- Viral Marketing Firm
- Business cards
- Fliers
- Website

Operation

Digital

Boss

By: Marquise Rodgers

Published by: Dropbackdistro

www.ingramcontent.com/pod-product-compliance
Lightning Source LLC
Chambersburg PA
CBHW070720210526
45170CB00021B/1387